LET'S WORK IT OUT™

What to Do When Your Parent Is Out of Work

Rachel Lynette

PowerKiDS press™

New York

Published in 2010 by The Rosen Publishing Group, Inc.
29 East 21st Street, New York, NY 10010

First Edition

Editor: Joanne Randolph
Layout Design: Julio Gil
Photo Researcher: Jessica Gerweck

Photo Credits: Cover © SuperStock/age fotostock; p. 4 Stan Honda/AFP/Getty Images; p. 6 © Jeff Greenberg/age fotostock; p. 8 © iStockphoto.com/Carmen Martínez Banús; p. 10 Scott Olson/ Getty Images; p. 12 © iStockphoto.com/Elena Elisseeva; p. 14 Leander Baerenz/Getty Images; p. 16 Marc Debnam/Getty Images; pp. 18, 20 Shutterstock.com.

Library of Congress Cataloging-in-Publication Data

Lynette, Rachel.
  What to do when your parent is out of work / Rachel Lynette. — 1st ed.
    p. cm. — (Let's work it out)
  Includes index.
  ISBN 978-1-4358-9338-2 (library binding) — ISBN 978-1-4358-9764-9 (pbk.) — ISBN 978-1-4358-9765-6 (6-pack)
  1. Children of unemployed parents—United States—Juvenile literature. 2. Unemployed—Services for—United States—Juvenile literature. I. Title.
  HD5724.L96 2010
  331.13'7—dc22
                                    2009023067

Manufactured in the United States of America

CPSIA Compliance Information: Batch #WW10PK: For Further Information contact Rosen Publishing, New York, New York at 1-800-237-9932

Contents

Sometimes businesses close down because they are not making enough money. This puts people out of work.

Unemployed

Most of the things that we need and want cost money. The clothes you are wearing cost money. The food you eat costs money. Even this book costs money! Most adults earn money by working at a job. Someone who has a job is **employed**. If one or both of your parents are employed, your family likely has enough money to buy many of the things it needs.

Sometimes, a parent loses his job. A person who does not have a job is **unemployed**. People who are unemployed often do not have enough money. Luckily, most people are not unemployed for very long.

Some people cannot work because they become disabled. Even with a disability, your parent is still there for you and your family.

How Did This Happen?

There are many reasons a person might lose her job. Sometimes a person is laid off. A person gets laid off because her **employer** no longer needs her. This may happen because the business closes or gets smaller. Sometimes new machines or computers do jobs that people used to do.

Sometimes people quit their jobs. A person may quit his job because he got hurt or very sick. Sometimes people quit because they do not like something about the job. Maybe it is too far away. Maybe it does not pay them enough money. People who quit usually try to get better jobs.

Offering to help around the house can lessen some of your parents' stress. Doing what you can to help your family will make you feel better, too.

Helping the Stress

If your parent loses her job, she may feel sad and angry. Your parent may feel that she was treated unfairly. She may feel like she should have done better. She may also be worried about money and about getting a new job. All these feelings can make your parents feel worried and **stressed**. This might make you feel worried and stressed, too.

People who are stressed often get angry easily. If your parents seem angry all the time or are yelling more often, try to remember that they are going through a hard time. Try not to let your feelings get hurt. Try your best not to get angry back. What can you do to help them feel better?

These people are waiting outside the unemployment office, where a job fair is being held. The office helps people without jobs find new ones.

Collecting Unemployment

When people work at a job, a small amount of money is taken out of each paycheck and put into a special **fund**. The money in this fund is used to make unemployment payments. Unemployment payments are made when a person loses his job.

If your parent loses his job, he may be able to collect unemployment. Your parent will have to apply for unemployment in order to collect payments. In most states, unemployment payments are about half the amount that your parent made when he was working. Unemployment will likely not be enough to pay for everything your family needs, but it can really help!

When unemployment runs out, your parent
may seem even more stressed.

When Unemployment Runs Out

In most states, people can collect unemployment payments for about six months. Many people find a new job before their unemployment payments run out. However, sometimes a person cannot find a new job in six months.

If your parent's unemployment runs out, your family may have to go on **welfare**. Welfare is a group of **government** programs that help families in need. Welfare programs can help your family by giving money, food, and help with housing and medical care. Welfare payments are not very much, but they can help your family get by until your parent has found a new job.

Your mom may need to find a quiet place to look in the newspaper or on the Internet for job openings.

On the Hunt

Looking for a new job is hard work! A person who is job hunting needs to spend a lot of time looking for job openings. He needs to write letters and make calls. He needs to have **interviews** with employers who might want to hire him. He may also need to take classes to learn new job skills.

Your parent may not have much time to spend with your family while she is job hunting. She may not have time to eat dinner with the family or help you with your homework. Try to be patient. It will not always be like this. Your parent is working hard to get your family back on its feet.

Moving in with relatives can be hard. If you stay positive, you may find that living with a grandparent can be lots of fun.

Make the Most of It

Hopefully, your parent will find a new job quickly. However, it might take longer than your parents had expected. If that happens, your parents will have to make a plan about how to pay for housing, food, and other things your family needs. The plan might mean that you have to give up things you enjoy or even move to a smaller house or apartment. You may even have to move in with your relatives for a while.

You are an important part of your family's plan. You can help by having a positive **attitude**, even when times are hard. Try not to complain. Find positive things to say instead. A positive attitude can make a big difference!

Instead of going to the movies, you and your parent might have fun reading a new library book.

A Time for Changes

A lot of things can change when a parent is out of work. There may not be enough money for new clothes or your favorite foods. You may have to wear secondhand clothes. You may have to get food from a **food bank**. It can help to remember that you will have to do these things only for a little while.

There may not be enough money to do fun things such as going to the movies or the arcade. What can you do instead? How about watching a video at home or playing a board game? There are many ways to have fun without spending money. This could be a great time to do things together as a family!

Talking to your parent can help you feel better. Try to explain how you feel openly and without complaining.

Talk About It

Even if you are trying to stay positive, you likely have a lot of feelings about your parent being out of work. You may feel worried, scared, sad, or even angry. It is okay to have those feelings, but it is not a good idea to keep them inside. Talking about your feelings can help you feel better.

Whom can you talk to? Talking to your parents can help. They may tell you things that will help you worry less. You might also want to talk to your friends. If you are feeling very sad or angry, you should talk to a **counselor**. A counselor can help you deal with strong feelings.

You Are Not Alone

A lot of times when one company is having trouble, other ones are, too. Sometimes so many businesses are having trouble it is called a **recession**. When the country is in a recession, a lot of people do not have jobs. That means that your family is not the only one struggling. Thousands of families are having some of the same problems you are!

The good news is that recessions do not usually last very long. Soon there will be more jobs. There are things you can do right now to help your parents. Find ways to help out around the house. Have a positive attitude. Someday soon, your parent will get a new job and things will be better!

Glossary

attitude (AH-tih-tood) A person's outlook or position.

counselor (KOWN-seh-ler) Someone who talks with people about their feelings and problems.

employed (im-PLOYD) Paid to work.

employer (im-PLOY-er) A person or a business that hires one or more people for wages.

food bank (FOOD BANGK) A place where people in need can get food to eat.

fund (FUND) Money that is saved to be used for a certain thing.

government (GUH-vern-mint) The people who make laws and run a state or a country.

interviews (IN-ter-vyooz) Meetings where someone questions someone else.

recession (rih-SEH-shun) A time when many businesses close and people are laid off.

stressed (STREST) Worried or feeling bad because of a problem.

unemployed (un-em-PLOYD) Without a job.

welfare (WEL-fer) Programs that give help to poor people.

Index

Web Sites

Due to the changing nature of Internet links, PowerKids Press has developed an online list of Web sites related to the subject of this book. This site is updated regularly. Please use this link to access the list:

www.powerkidslinks.com/lwio/work/